Swimwear in VOGUE

Swimwear *in* VOGUE

SINCE 1910

by Christina Probert

ABBEVILLE PRESS · PUBLISHERS · NEW YORK

ACKNOWLEDGMENTS

So many people have shared their talents with *Vogue* over the years: artists, photographers, designers, craftsmen, writers, but also *Vogue*'s own editors whose perspicacious choices have shaped the magazine. I am indebted to Alex Kroll, Editor of Condé Nast Books, for his guidance throughout, Georgina Boosey for her editorial wisdom, Liz Bauwens for the book's design, Trudy Lee for her advice and ever-present help.

C.P.

Library of Congress catalog card number 81-67879

ISBN 0–89659–242–1

Cover. BV 1976 Peccinotti. Back Cover. BV 1922 Ann Fish. Page 2. BV 1976 Barry Lategan. *Isidore*

CONTENTS

Key to captions

Information is given in the following order: edition; year; artist or photographer; designer or maker (the last always in *italic*). Editions are identified by initials:

AV   American *Vogue*
BV   British *Vogue*
FV   French *Vogue*
IV   Italian *Vogue*
GV   German *Vogue*

INTRODUCTION

Think but of the surprise of his majesty when,
the first time of his bathing, he had no sooner popped
his royal head under water than a band of music,
concealed in a neighbouring machine,
struck up 'God save great George our King'.
Fanny Burney's diary for 1789.

Brave George III was surrounded by 'loyal nymphs', clad in tucked-up flannel dresses with bandeaux and girdles, bonnets bearing the loyal motto. The whole appeared so singular to Fanny Burney that 'it was with some difficulty that I kept my features in order'. For George, in sea-bathing, was not following a fashion but inadvertently creating one. 'Taking the waters' – bathing in, or drinking large quantities of, often unpleasant mineral water – had long been a fashionable pastime and an aid to health. Swimming did not enjoy the same favour in the West, after the fall of the Roman Empire, until the twentieth century. Strange indeed, for while swimming is not natural to man, he seems always to have enjoyed dipping in streams and coves.

It was for medicinal reasons that the fashionable took to sea water. In the nineteenth century, sea bathing from 'bathing machines' became popular, involving immersion, but not swimming, in the briny deep, clad in heavy silk or woollen garments, as a cure for many illnesses. While George III's mental problems were probably aggravated by the shock of the icy water, hydrotherapy is still widely used to alleviate pain from rheumatic and arthritic complaints, and salt water is particularly supportive to the body. Special clothing gradually evolved, to allow more movement to the bather, though weighty costumes still hampered the would-be swimmer until well into the twentieth century.

The swimmer was not a member of the fashionable set until 1910. Swimming, as violent exercise, was still not socially acceptable for modish women in 1900; on land, too, their tightly laced corsets and voluminous petticoats restricted their movements, and soft elegance, not fitness, was the 'look'. Swimming costumes were thus not fashionable essentials at the beginning of the century, and until the First World War *Vogue* carried very few editorials on the subject. The stores advertised costumes, but they were drab in colour and cut; in 1913 *Vogue* itself produced patterns for do-it-yourself costumes, to meet the 'distinct need for smart bathing costumes'. The War changed attitudes towards women doing physical work: 1914 proved to be

Vast cape, turban, flowing dress, wool-clad legs, lace-up pumps: the outfit for the seaside before the First World War. A V 1912 Helen Dryden

1910

Seascape-appliquéd cape, hat, parasol.
A V 1917 D.M. Tighe

Sashed satin suit.
A V 1914

a watershed in women's lives. The War effort changed lifestyles overnight, fashions changed dramatically – and suddenly swimwear *was* fashion.

'It took', said *Vogue*, 'a certain amount of courage for the bathing-girl to appear in this daring costume, and she really deserves the credit for firing the first shot in the Battle of Modern Dress.' Swimwear editorials now appeared regularly in *Vogue*, like 1914's 'Beach fashions at high water-mark – bathing suits that follow fashion's latest fads'. No longer was it a difficult task to choose pretty beach clothes.

After the War, society's gaze turned once again to travel. Deauville's season lengthened now, and Le Touquet became a popular resort for the international set. Until 1920 the south of France had enjoyed only a winter season, mainly patronized by the old and infirm. Now that better cars and the *Train bleu* made the Midi more accessible, Cannes, Menton – and the Venice Lido too – became part of the season. In the United States, where East Coast summer weather was almost as reliable as that on the Côte d'Azur, an appearance on Palm Beach (or Long Beach) was essential for the *bon ton*. Quite naturally swimming came to augment the other seaside pleasures of tea on the terrace, the casino and dancing. Bathing costumes became more streamlined and thus easier to swim in, but generally were still designed for parading and paddling. It was not until the following decade that the idea of swimming for health, for a fitter body, gained popularity, as personality and fashion photographs taken *in situ* testify.

The shape of swimwear follows the fashionable silhouette for outerwear. Thus in 1910, when the 'pouter pigeon' chest shape was the mode, swimming costumes followed suit, giving a rather bolstered and solid outline. Very little flesh was exposed; the costume was a knee-length dress with pleated or flared skirt to allow movement when wet, sometimes long-sleeved for the 'bather who fears sunburn', but more often cut with short sleeves. Necklines were cut in a high square, or with a collar in Gladstone (turned up at the back, with little points at the front) or sailor style. This rather hefty garment was worn with black woollen or silk stockings and little pumps, often with lacing up the leg. The frilled and flounced costumes of 1914 were both physically and aesthetically lighter. Shorter now, with bloomers (also known as pantalets, pantalons) daring to show themselves, these costumes caused *Vogue* to warn that 'to be good taste, to be sure, bathing suits must necessarily be conservative in effect'. Open necks were the fashion of the 1914 season, with little white piqué collars, waists were increasingly sashed, often in bright colours.

As the decade progressed, skirts, bloomers and sleeves got shorter, and by 1918 sleeveless costumes were being worn in far brighter colours than had been permissible in 1910. More daring still was the knitted, woollen, striped one-piece which appeared in 1918, reaching to the knee and buttoned down the legs and side. It was so avant-garde that it had to be worn with a little wrapover dress, discarded only at the water's edge. Costumes were now less shaped, sashes went out of fashion, and the long, lean look gained ground. Some costumes still had a waistline marked with edging or contrasting detail; piping, fringing, ribbon edgings, became the focal point of the costume.

A modish costume alone was by no means enough to gain access to the smartest bathing *plages*. The fashionable paraded the sands hung around with parasols (essential beach accessory after 1914), brightly embroidered beach bags, ever larger swirling capes, often of rubberized silks in bright prints, with contrast edging. Girdles were essential until mid-decade, too, in spotted taffeta, rubber, patent leather.

Swimming hats began the decade as large, impractical, cap-like or turbanned objects. Later versions were fitted to the head, in rubberized fabric or plain satin, sometimes chin-strapped, when destined for the waves. They served to keep hair tidy but also to conform with etiquette's ruling that hats should be worn outside. Perhaps surprisingly, the latter seems to have been the real *causa* for the use of swimhats over several decades; for when, in the late sixties, hats ceased to be everyday wear, swimhats ceased to be the norm too. Shoes were an essential. Earliest were pumps, with or without the leg lacing which reappears spasmodically in twentieth-century shoe fashion. Made of satin or kid, they were worn with dark stockings of wool or silk. By the end of the decade stockings had become optional when the new boots were worn. There were two versions, either slip-on style, reaching just above the ankle, or longer still, laced up the front: neither seems at all practical for swimming!

Costume colours and fabrics were very limited in 1910. Satin was the most widely used, chiefly in black, also in dark brown, dark blue and plum. Silk can change colour when wet: Gimbel Brothers advertised their 'salt-waterproof silks . . . guaranteed to withstand the ravages of the deep'. Less heavy and severe fabrics followed: taffeta became a top favourite, and by mid-decade silk moiré, crepe de chine, charmeuse and wool jersey had become as widely used as satin. By 1917 rubberized fabrics had arrived and promptly became a craze for every beach necessity: bags, hats, capes, belts, bandannas were all made in rubberized silks. Rubber flowers were popular. Fashionable beach accessories were thematically linked, with appliquéd land- and seascapes.

By 1920 a beach outfit was vital to every wardrobe. It was an ensemble demanding as much planning and care as one for the Ascot races, and equally lively. For swimming, sunning, *tête à tête*, the ensemble was versatile, no longer something to be donned for paddling and swiftly removed in favour of something more fashionable. 'Far greater latitude than ever before seems to have been given to the designers of bathing suits' said *Vogue*, 'and they have taken advantage of it.'

The changing silhouette, lighter, briefer, in line with street fashion. BV 1919

1920

AV 1910 Helen Dryden

BV 1918

AV 1914 Helen Dryden

AV 1913 E.M.I. Steinmetz

The swimwear of 1910, *opposite*,
exposed very little to the elements;
the costume, right of the group, was
designed for 'the bather who fears
sunburn': protection, in black silk,
from the dreaded rays. The others
are of black silk too, one with piped
cord decoration, the other in nautical
style: thick stockings of wool or silk
complete coverage. Later styles, *left*,
from 1913 are lighter and shorter:
'following the street fashion of
frivolously frilled frocks', but still of
heavy silk, with a weighty patent
cummerbund. The suit, *above*, from
1914, has a much lighter appearance,
intended for swimming, not just
sunbasking: 'above the blue of the
suit "breaks" the white collar', said
Vogue. The 1917 suit for 'a smart
appearance on the sand and the fun of
a good swim', *top left*, under the
parasol.

BV 1919 Claire Avery

BV 1919 Such. *Marshall & Snelgrove*

'Bathing suits have decided to keep pace with fashion, step by step,
and so go in for sashes, embroidery, and odd colour combinations.'
By the end of the First World War a huge variety of styles and
colours were available in swimwear. Bloomers, now on show, were
often used as part of the whole design, in contrasting fabric, *opposite
below left*, or trimmed to match, *opposite above and below*, *this page
above*. Many suits were sleeveless, skirts shorter, the waist marked
only by loose sashes, or contrast piping; the look was long, lean,
emphasis on detail and not a fussy outline. Worn with all these were
lace-up shoes or boots, small turbans, pill-box hats. Most daring suit
was this, *right*, of fine, clinging, striped wool jersey in one piece,
its protean talent hidden right to the water's edge by a slip-on surplice
bodice and skirt of black and white silk.

BV 1918

Palm beach 1917: the smart set at play. *Left*, Philadelphian family, the Wideners, in the latest beach attire: mother in black taffeta dress with scalloped hem, her daughter in a softer jersey suit.

Miss Audrey Osborn, *centre left*, in dark-hued costume of taffeta, belted with bright sash; *centre right*, Miss Rosamond Lancaster in the season's new fabric, rubberized corduroy. Shiny silk satin, *left*, worn by Miss Natalie Johnson, with large, soft hat, ankle-tied shoes.

'This wrap, *left*, is the sort of thing that Diana, or any of those athletic Olympian girls, would have just loved to toss on after a strenuous dash around Parnassus. It's of old-rose tussore silk, long and roomy, with rose and green leaves on back and collar.' Another version, *below*, of blue wool jersey and rubberized satin.

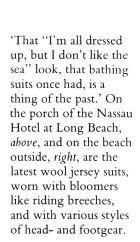

'That "I'm all dressed up, but I don't like the sea" look, that bathing suits once had, is a thing of the past.' On the porch of the Nassau Hotel at Long Beach, *above*, and on the beach outside, *right*, are the latest wool jersey suits, worn with bloomers like riding breeches, and with various styles of head- and footgear.

1920

'The modern girl is triumphant. She can wear anything she wants to wear, but, if she is wise, she will be careful not to let her freedom go to her head. After all, a bathing suit tells a more honest story than any other form of dress. . . .' The bulky silhouette of the previous decade's costumes had gone; the new suits were long, lean, exposing more skin to the sun's rays every season, looking increasingly like the male maillot. This suit, with vest-shaped top and shorts reaching to ankle and later knee, had been male swimming fashion for decades, while women were still paddling in dresses. Now, for women too, the body was on show at all the smartest beaches, clad in the newest, knitted, clinging fabrics. Beaches were a very important part of summer life. By mid-decade the smart world was not content merely to dash to the beach for a swim before luncheon, but went 'equipped for long, leisurely hours in the water and on the sands, with parasols and cushions, chairs and bags, and a wide variety of costumes to add to the comfort of all concerned.' The fashionable resorts were developed, terraces built down to attractive cove beaches, parades along level beaches, umbrella'd shady spots provided for those with *coup de soleil*, night spots for the young and lively.

Such activity required an extensive wardrobe. Two-piece tubular costumes were worn at the beginning of the decade, a long top with loosely fitting shorts emphasizing the hip line. The simplicity of this line was an innovation, but 'might be just as attractive as the more ornate dresses when it has unexpected stripes in bright colours', reassured *Vogue*. Top and shorts matched or contrasted, tops were often of printed fabric, shorts plain: Patou produced Chinese prints mid-decade, a crop of angular, crowded and often geometric prints on crepe de chine followed.

As the transition from fuller to fitting costumes was made, cover-ups in the form of capes, shawls and coats became essential fashion items. Ann Fish commented on this in her humorous drawings of 1922 (see pp. 20–21): maidens leap through the foam, clad in tiny costumes kept almost invisible by vast swirls of cape! Beachwear attained a more tailored appearance; coats matched costumes in length and breadth. Mid-decade there was a throwback to a wider, balloon-like shape, following the same movement in everyday wear, but it was brief-lived; for, as *Vogue* said, 'the newest thing for the sea is a jersey bathing suit as near a maillot as the unwritten law will permit'.

The one-piece suit of the late twenties was daring, but the greatest novelty on the beach was the pyjama suit which was introduced in 1927. Not only was this a completely new shape for women to wear: as these garments were not governed by old-established rules of etiquette, considerable liberty could be taken in the choice of colours and fabrics. But, warned *Vogue*, 'let good taste set the rules'. Very bright Oriental prints appeared at first, but, as pyjamas were incorporated into the whole beach ensemble, their colourings were chosen to tone with the whole. By 1930 these suits were often

Green, yellow and pastel-blue striped suit: shorter, slimmer, with parasol and cloche-like cap.
BV 1922. *Peter Robinson*

16

bias-cut, always tailored, and made of fabrics like crepe de chine, éponge (the earliest towelling), jersey.

'To burn or not to burn' was the hottest summer question of the decade. At first it was fashionable to prostrate oneself on the beach, clad in the new shorter costumes, regardless of the dangers involved. Later in the decade, beauty house advertisements, and editorials too, began to warn of the long-term dangers to the skin of sunburn: the extent of the danger had increased as costumes got smaller, even backless and exposing all the shoulder area. New, too, was the idea that the body inside the swimming costume should look fit, and that 'certain types of suits are more appropriate than others', depending on the shape to be clad. 'Whether to swim at all is a consideration', said *Vogue* in 1923, 'for swimming has a way of increasing the girth in an amazingly short time.' By 1930 the smartest suit was that of masculine simplicity and brevity, a utilitarian suit that 'does not look like a feminine frock'.

Perhaps the most important beach accessory in the twenties was a capacious, rubber-lined holdall. Patou's version was of canvas awning fabric, big enough to contain a whole summer's wardrobe! Beach hats gradually divided into swimming and sunning hats. Hats for swimming, like the cloche, were tight fitting, curved around the temples, often designed to allow a few escaping shingled waves to frame the face. Large-brimmed straws were the vogue for strolling the sands in, sometimes with fringed edges. Towels were large, too, woven with stripes and geometric designs to match costumes. Shoes were flat, of rubber or canvas; Schiaparelli produced stripy socks for the beach. The flowing capes of the previous decade continued into the early twenties; shawls followed, then coats with the tailored look: these became the most popular cover-up, worn with pyjamas and swimsuits.

Stripes, swirls, chevrons, circles, dots, squares and triangles: all these bold and geometric shapes, in appliqué or print, were popular in the twenties. Cubism too influenced dress; French *Vogue* showed *foulards cubistes* to wrap around costumes. Colours for the whole ensemble were white with black or dark tones like ruby, deep blue; alternatively contrasting brights were used together, orange with jade, scarlet with yellow. The newest fabrics were jerseys: heavy for coats and capes, lighter for swimsuits in wool, silk, linen and cotton (these known as tricot or stockingette). For the sands there were crepe de chine, printed silks, linen, shirting, éponge, even cashmere.

'Since the inspiration of our couturiers found new ground for expression in bathing creations, time spent on fashionable beaches has become the most exhilarating of the day.' For on the beach one could, as *Vogue* noted, relax completely, behave exactly as one wished. In clothes, too, there was great leeway for self-expression, resulting in 'the most fantastic arrangements of garments' coming into fashion.

Arbiter of the mode. A V 1927. A.E. Marty

Princesse J.-L. de Faucigny-Lucinge, always at the forefront of fashion, here in bright swimsuit, nautical hat. F V 1927

1930

BV 1921. *Astoria*

BV 1921 Helen Dryden

'Since black satin has taken to the water as kindly as any duckling, this pretty and practical costume, *opposite*, is made of that material, with a trimming of black and white striped satin, and a cap of water-proofed black satin. The wrap on the left is of heavy grey sponge cloth with tasselled cord.' Suit of sky blue tricot, *right*, trimmed with red soutache at shoulder, knee.

BV 1921. *Astoria*

'On land, the lady on the left, *above*, has a decidedly celestial air, but in the water she becomes a vivid goldfish, because of the glowing orange satin of her bathing suit. The bands of turquoise blue are guarded by narrow ones of black, and blue tassels end the sash. Her companion would look like a delectable raspberry in her soft Canton crepe suit, but for the darker bands.'

'Aphrodite rising from the foam may have been dazzlingly beautiful, but these three graces are convinced that foam as a decorative adjunct may be overdone. They are far more inclined to place their confidence in gorgeous bathing cloaks, flung about them in seagoing fashion.'

'That Madame prefers her smart wrap of black and white stripes, *left*, to the more brilliant cover-alls of her neighbours, *right*, is a matter she makes no attempt at all to disguise. But then, with an aristocratic nose like hers, one must find something to look down.'

20

BV 1922 Ann Fish

BV 1922 Ann Fish

'Gone are the days when a bathing suit was simply a covering that would wring out well. To-day, one's individuality must be considered.' Various interpretations of the black and white geometric mode, *above, left and right*. Beach tents, *below*, for the slender and the over-endowed, respectively.

The long, lean look: tubular trunks and tops on masculine lines, undersuits and wrapover tops, maillots. Patou's designs, *opposite*, are bright, like the suit *far left*, in orange crepe marocain with white appliquéd patterns, or black and white, like his one-piece manlike suit for the energetic swimmer. The flowing cape, smart since the onset of revealing suits, is still *à la mode*, but in lighter fabrics. Patou's third suit, like those *on this page*, is Chinese-influenced, with its Mandarin neckline, side-buttoning, slightly flared skirt. The clear, bright prints, on silk pongee and crepe de chine, *on this page* are Chinese in clarity of printing, colouring too, deep and sapphire blue with white and ivory, but Western in the geometric fabric design and cut. With them are worn jersey undersuits, little turbans, strapped pumps and rubberized beach capes like this one, *above right*, of natural silk printed with vivid kaleidoscopic patterns.

A V 1924 L. Fellows. *Bonwit Teller, Simon*

A V 1924 L. Fellows. *Franklin Simon*

A V 1924 L. Fellows. *Bonwit Teller*

23

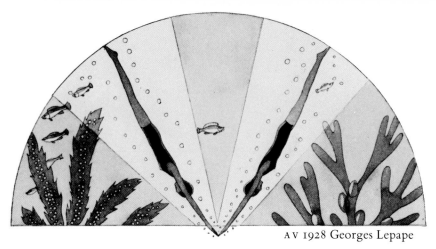

A V 1928 Georges Lepape

24 A V 1927 Harriet Meserole. *Left to right: Saks–Fifth Avenue, Bonwit Teller, Best, Saks–Fifth Avenue, Best, Bonwit Teller*

Soleil, Soleil..!

FV 1927

Beaches, by the mid-twenties, had become a very important part of smart summer life; the fashionable went to the beach equipped for long, leisurely hours on the sands. The vast beach-bag, *this page right*, was perhaps the most important accessory of all, being the bearer of everything a swimmer could require. It might contain a variety of swimsuits: a slimline maillot, *opposite above*, for violent swimming, a maillot with low back, *above*, for dipping and sunning, a softer style for sunbathing, *right*. For moments of conversation with one's friends, parasols, large straw sunhats, various kinds of cover-ups were necessary: beach pyjamas, two styles *right*, were the latest covered-up beachwear of 1928. The long coat of the pyjama suit could also be worn with the bathing dress, as *opposite*, 'to the water's edge to prevent sunburn, and perhaps as some last vestige of modesty'. The smartest straw hats now have fringes.

A V 1928 Pierre Mourgue.
Left to right: Schiaparelli, Lelong, Lord & Taylor

25

BV 1927.
Lee Erick
Jean Pato

Lee Creelman Erickson

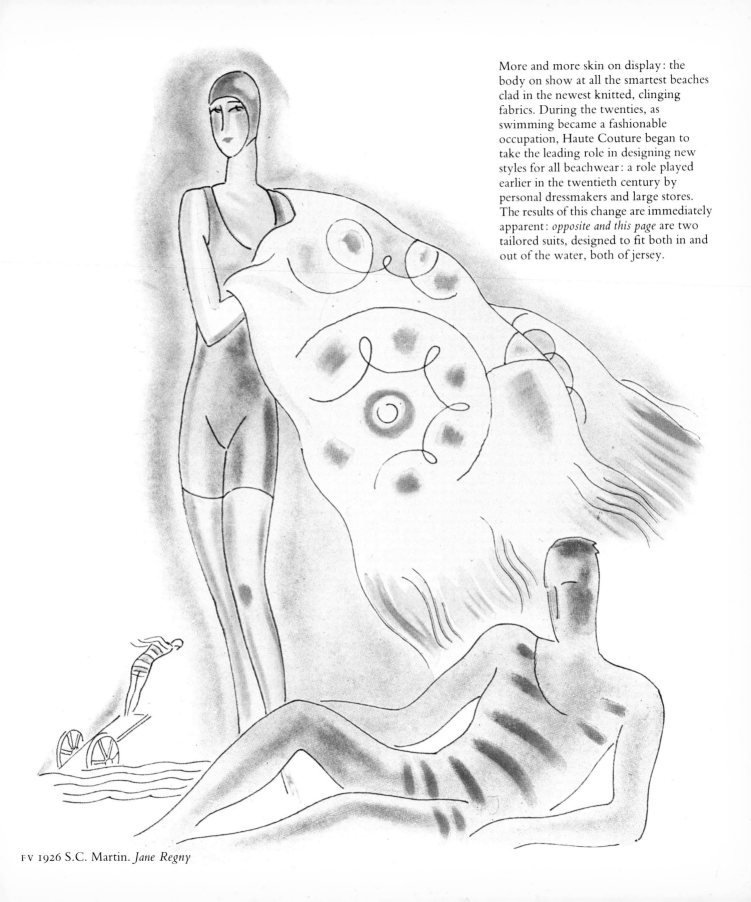

More and more skin on display: the body on show at all the smartest beaches clad in the newest knitted, clinging fabrics. During the twenties, as swimming became a fashionable occupation, Haute Couture began to take the leading role in designing new styles for all beachwear: a role played earlier in the twentieth century by personal dressmakers and large stores. The results of this change are immediately apparent: *opposite and this page* are two tailored suits, designed to fit both in and out of the water, both of jersey.

FV 1926 S.C. Martin. *Jane Regny*

FV 1928 Hoyningen-Huené. *Beer*

FV 1928 Hoyningen-Huené. *Jeanne Lanvin*

Haute Couture designs for summer 1928: swimwear editorials like this had become the norm in all *Vogue*'s editions. Patou, *opposite*, and Lanvin, *above*, were both using patterned jerseys with toning plain knits for two-piece suits. Schiaparelli's suit, *right*, had matching stripy top and socks, plain shorts. *Top, this page*, Beer used triangles of silk for cape and swimsuit. Colours for the season were strongly contrasting duos.

928 Hoyningen-Huené. *Jean Patou*

FV 1928 Hoyningen-Huené. *Schiaparelli*

1930

'There is something in the blood of human beings – especially women, but men too – which makes them feel that if only they could be lying under the sun in a minimum of clothes, preferably with blue water in the foreground, everything would automatically be all right.' The preparation attached to such relaxation was extensive, as the rites and manners involved in the 'Undressed Life' became still more complex during the thirties. No longer could the fashionable sunbathe without spending the requisite amount of time exercising (especially with the Michelin push-ball), swimming, diving, sunning – and without ensuring that they were wearing the right brand of sun preparation. 'For instance,' said American *Vogue*, 'you certainly don't use oil when you are lying about on your host's deck getting a sunburn, because, if you did, you would ruin the lovely, lovely deck, and the punishment for ruining a deck is usually something like being blown from the mouth of a cannon or walking the plank.'

Fitness was the craze now: British *Vogue* published an article on swimming-pools within easy reach of London, listing their amenities for sociable evening dips, so fashionable was this form of exercise. Costumes became smaller, tighter and more revealing, the body inside needed to look trimmer: the appearance of Lastex and Contralex, fabrics with elastic woven into them, meant that even the bulgy could appear slender in their swimming outfits. Photography of swimwear was far from static. Toni Frissell was one of a new breed of photographers who laid great emphasis on health and vitality as well as fashion in their work.

The bathing maillot was 'summer underwear', the basis of most summer beach-and-bathing combinations. Some costumes were still two overlapping pieces, but the most popular were all in one, at first white or pale, later bright. The top of the costume was increasingly low-cut at the front, lower still at the back, even backless. Mid-decade much effort was put into designing a costume back which allowed maximum exposure to the sun and yet maximum comfort while swimming: cross straps, which could be removed while sunbathing under the new sunlamps or on the beach, became popular on low-backed suits.

In 1935 the 'bikini' (not known by this name until after the hydrogen bomb on Bikini Atoll in 1946) appeared on *Vogue*'s pages. It was a swimming suit which left some inches of flesh exposed between its two parts. Some wore

Mainbocher's bicycle beach suit, *top left*, with other variations on beach sportswear. A V 1935. *Mainbocher (both standing), Anivo*

it, but the bared midriff did not become a fashion essential until 1940. The hips were now the focal point of the maillot, for while the cut changed little from 1935 to 1940, maillots became tighter. The curve of the hips was emphasized, both by the straight line with which the costume ended over the thigh, and by the accompanying inward pull of the elastic fabric.

Other forms of beach two-piece were high fashion in the thirties. The more versatile playsuit or beach suit had ousted pyjamas from their popularity: 'slip on a beach suit instead of a pyjama,' said *Vogue*, 'it's newer'. This could consist of shorts and top, skirt and top, or, more unusually, trousers and top, in matching fabric. The décolletage of the top followed the line of the maillot underneath: a halter shape with low back was worn throughout the decade. The 'bicycle beach suit' (baggy bloomers and long sleeved jumper in wool) became a great craze with the health-conscious. Loose trousers were generally popular early in the decade to wear over the maillot, as were little skirts or shorts, gathered or wrapover, for walks along the promenade or to the shops. All these beach-and-bathing co-ordinates came to be tailored like street clothes as 1940 approached.

More tailored, too, were the hip-length beach coats and capes. Hats for sunning were huge and flat, of rigid or softer straw, but without the curved brims of the twenties. 'Peon' hats and clothes came briefly into fashion, and this mood influenced millinery for more than a decade, producing vast cartwheel hats held on with a ribbon under the chin. Beach shoes were sandals, with little heels for walking on the promenade, flatter for the sands, sometimes with leg lacing: playsuits often had matching fabric sandals. Hats, shoes, tailored separates all teamed to create a chic whole: dressing, not undressing, was the beach mode by mid-decade.

The most important new fabric was the elasticated knit: patterned or plain, it made the swimming costume really body-shaped. Important, too, was terry cloth, a spongy cotton which looked like wool and was much more absorbent than the éponge of the previous decade. It was used for towels, beach robes, even beach playsuits. Cotton piqué, printed or plain, toile, glazed chintz, knits in various fibres, were used for playsuits and accessories. At least one white swimming costume was an essential in the early thirties, and white shorts, skirts, trousers were also favourites. White maillots were worn with bright skirts and shorts, linen playsuits or trousers with bright coats and scarves. Later, bright colours took over, particularly brilliant and brash prints in scarlet, blue, green, yellow, perhaps with white.

Whether clad only in a maillot, or dressed up in skirt, top and coat, a fit, trim body was the emphasis of all these clothes. As *Vogue* said mid-decade: 'the new jersey adheres to you like a new and handsome skin, and the couturiers are cutting all the bathing suits completely on the cross, which goes a long way towards making them cling to you like mad'.

New, short beach cape and sandals. A V 1936 Christian Bérard. *Bérard/Bonwit Teller*

Playsuit of embroidered linen top and plain shorts. A V 1934 Cecil Beaton. *James McCutcheon*

1940

AV 1930 Hoyningen-Huené. *Left to right: Hélène Yrande (2), Jean d'Ahetze*

opposite top
AV 1930 Hoyningen-Huené. *Left to right: Jean d'Ahetze (2), Jane Régny*

below left
FV 1931 Hoyningen-Huené. *Lucien Lelong*

below right
AV 1930 Hoyningen-Huené. *A.J. Izod*

32

The Michelin push-ball, popular for exercising in the fitness-crazy thirties, *above*. The back of the bathing maillot was now extremely low, often with (removable) straps to make violent swimming possible, *left*, and belts of oilcloth, *above*, or jersey, *opposite*, to draw in the waist and add colour to the ever-simpler suit. Playsuits, like the dungarees *opposite left*, have replaced the beach pyjamas of the twenties; these are in red breton sailcloth.

Idyllic summer life,
this page, yards out
in deep blue ocean,
clad in backless,
bright maillot, no
swimhat, with only
fish and ships to
take into considera-
tion. Strolling on
the sands, *opposite*,
protected from too
much sun in clothes
inspired by
traditions of the
Mediterranean
countries. *Left to
right*: Greek drape
of *toile de lin*,
Arabian bloused
pantaloons and
glazed chintz top
with umbrella hat,
Italian linen apron
and headdress,
Turkish white wool
draped pants and
bodice.

A V 1932

SUMMER
FASHIONS

JUNE · 1 · 1932
PRICE 35 CENTS
©THE CONDÉ NAST PUBLICATIONS, INC

A V 1930

A V 1934

B V 1932

I V 1931

B V 1932

All the smartest people in all the smartest places (American residents object to 'resorts'). Loretta Young, *above*, cool and sylph-like in her geometric, fine jersey suit; bathing beauties, *above right*, pose at Newport: Mrs Douglas, Mrs Cushing, Mrs Phipps, Mrs Stevens. Madame Georges Auric, *below them*, in the bicycle beach suit which took the Riviera by storm; also on the Riviera, *far right*, Lady Castlerosse and Madame Fabre-Luce, in man-tailored beach suit and maillot with skirt. *Below right*, the English scene: Miss Virginia Hutchinson in 'very tricky bathing dress'.

36

Partie de bain on the rocks near Madame Boissevain's Antibes villa: all are prepared for a lazy day, sun-oil at hand, the men in daringly brief suits, the women sunbathing in swimhats!

BV 1932

Fervid sun-worshippers: S.A.R. La Princesse Sixte de Bourbon-Parme, Madame Pereire and M. Ambericos, *left*, relax hatless, shoeless in the new low-backed swimsuits. *Right*, Madame Lucien Lelong and Serge Lifar exercising on the beach at Venice, she in baggy trousers.

FV 1931

FV 1931

BV 1932

BV 1932

The Comtesse Elie de Gaigneron testing the water, *far left*, in a ribbed jersey suit designed for active swimming, not mere dipping, with its firm cross straps. The Hon. Mrs Evelyn Fitzgerald, *left*, at the lido in 'the newest bathing dress', a wrapover top baring the back, little shorts.

37

Oilskin smock in new hip length. Scarf like a stock

Tips from jockeys: flannel culottes, striped shirts, visor caps

short-sleeves on a matelassé crêpe bathing-suit

Mademoiselle Chanel on the Lido — linen suit, pearls, enamel bracelets

Scotch cap, gingham play dress. Pierrot towelling cape

BV, AV 1936 Christian Bérard. *Left to right: Bérard, Jaeger/Bonwit Teller*

Undressing and dressing-up, the conflicting (but not mutually exclusive) beach modes of the mid- and late thirties. Vertès captioned his watercolour *opposite*: 'It's divine – but my husband hates *me* to wear such low necks', while drawing for *Vogue* the most shocking, semi-naked swimwear fashion shown in the magazine to date: tops are minuscule, shorts cut-away. Only the very daring adopted this look; most swimwear was far more covering. At the other end of the scale was the tailored, covered beach look, *this page*. As in all thirties swimwear, emphasis on the hip-line was strong, with hip-length smocks, jackets too, short full skirts flaring over the hip. With all these, round sunglasses, bangles and beads, heeled shoes.

Fashionable sports of the thirties, *both pages*, are shown with the most fashionable swimwear for each. Water skiing, *this page*, in *Vogue*'s earliest example of the suit later to be known as the bikini: it left several inches of midriff exposed. *Opposite, above left and right*, Norma Shearer exercising on the beach (she disliked swimming) and Miss Caroline Thompson, plotting to shoot a wave on her 'Li-Lo'. Both these swimsuits, and those *below left*, are of jersey woven with elastic, known as Lastex or Contralex, which made the suit fit better and hold in bulges. A more traditional fabric for the suit *below right*, alpaca with white cotton for the revers, poised on the edge of nowhere. Note the flattish shoes; American *Vogue* had this advice: 'may we exhort you not to wear highish-heeled beach shoes? They smack of news-reel beauty contests and somehow don't belong.'

F·V 1935 Pierre Walter

A V 1935 Toni Frissell

B V 1937 Paal

A V 1936 Steichen. *Saks–Fifth Avenue*

B V 1938 Toni Frissell. *Simpsons*

B V 1936 Steichen

B V 1937 Anton Bruehl

A V 1938

B V 19

A V 1934 Steichen

Vogue covers of the thirties, *this page* and small pictures *opposite*. Swimming was now such a popular sport that summer covers often carried examples of the latest swimwear. Not only the clothes were on show: the cover, *this page*, was captioned 'against a background of salt spray and glistening rocks . . . this girl just emerging from her dip, radiant with health, her skin tanned to a lovely brown all over, just as yours, too, can be if you want'. Main picture *opposite*, six young American residents picnicking on Waikiki beach in all the latest playsuits with halter necks, jersey swimsuits, stripy beach trousers.

B V 1937 Toni Frissell

1940

'We Americans love the sun. Thrive in the sun. Follow the sun, come cold weather, to California, Florida, Arizona, New Mexico. No wonder we're famous for our sun clothes.' (American *Vogue*, 1941.) Swimwear fashion continued to develop throughout the Second World War in the United States; the fashions produced were innovative and were to influence European post-war fashion. Until 1942 there was no fabric rationing; and the allowances, when they were imposed, were generous, as American *Vogue* noted: 'much less fabric than the law allows catches Vitamin D'.

The preoccupation was with creating the illusion of a year-round tan; for a tan had become a status symbol, even more so in wartime. 'Your first few days in a bathing suit won't look so First if you use a pseudo tan' ran an early forties advertisement in American *Vogue*. British *Vogue* had the following advice for its readers in 1942: 'With the tension of wartime living and the fatigue of wartime work . . . make the most of every opportunity to bask in the sun.' Not on the beach, of course: Britain's beaches were mined and fenced off for the duration of the War. Tans were more likely to be acquired while contributing to the War effort: digging potatoes or harvesting, for those in the country. For city-dwellers in Europe, getting into the sun was much more difficult.

After 1945, as beaches were opened and seaside holidays became possible again, 'sea, sun, a tan and the right look' became the recipe for an ideal post-war summer. Seaside clothes had, of necessity, become much simpler. The late thirties' multiple layers of, for example, maillot, skirt, shirt, coat, cape, had gone: even in the United States wartime fabric problems had precluded such a look. Instead, there were new, more 'dressed-up' swimsuits, brighter, printed, as well as the more streamlined and now traditional maillots.

'Beach dresses have become very short, in toile of linen, silk, jersey, cotton, buttoned across the ribs under an almost chaste sunbathing bodice, over a skirt with godets . . .' (French *Vogue*, 1948; godets are shaped fabric insertions to add fullness). Some of these dresses were suitable for the water, too: particularly those of cotton which held their shape when wet and dried quickly. 'Go bare-waisted,' said *Vogue*, 'on the laziest, sunniest days.' Bare midriff suits with draped skirts like mini-sarongs were very popular in the United States during the first half of the decade, and later came the 'irreducable minimum': bra top with thin straps, slightly cutaway knickers with a shaped hemline around the thigh to flatter the leg. The Leg Look was in; and *Vogue* considered that even sturdy legs were acceptable if they were brown and firm. The ever-popular one-piece costume was frillier, ruched, much more feminine. The bust was usually padded out or underwired, depending on the figure inside: American *Vogue* showed a 'strapless suit, bared to the 24th vertebra, wired to hug the ribs, ruched all over'. American *Vogue* also gave advice on how to choose between all these options: 'Don't spoil the

'Strapless suit, bared to the 24th vertebra.' A V 1948 George Platt Lynes. *Cole of California*

The bare-waisted ballerina skirt. A V 1940 Bolin. *Altman*

looks of your perfect dive with a fluffy-ruffles, cutie-pie suit . . . don't go in for violent water sports in a suit with trick fastenings . . . don't fail to make a campaign of buying your bathing suit, take off your girdle before you try on for it's likely to give you delusions of grandeur about your figure . . . don't overdo the little-girl angle when you are chronologically or anatomically unsuited . . . don't stop at *one* bathing suit. . . .'

Full skirts and narrow trousers were the most popular beach cover-ups. Trousers were generally shorter, often ending well above the ankle. Skirts, on the other hand, were full, flared, pleated or gathered, to the knee or ballerina length (the most popular of all). Shorts were worn too, their popularity enhanced by fabric economies. Tailored jackets in bright contrasting colours, to go with all these, appeared after the War. Beach hats went out of fashion, and scarves, headbands and turbans were worn instead, further obvious examples of the War's effect on fashion. Beach shoes were not emphasized by fashion, either: many of *Vogue*'s models appeared barefoot, and only the minority wore rope-soled, fabric sand shoes.

'Plunge into colour. It plays up white. It plays up you. Splash into the surf in pale blue, sea-shell pink, water-green, sunny yellow – make a dive for stripes.' American wartime costumes were bright, influenced by the *avant-garde* costumes of California (for some time now a fashionable year-round sunning spot). After the War, too, brilliants were popular, to counteract the drab styles of previous years. Polynesian and Mexican prints began to gain popularity in Europe and the United States, also plain colours with printed or contrasting borders. Rayon was very widely used, often in crepe for swimsuits, also in sharkskin; elasticated jersey was the norm for one-piece swimsuits: waffled piqué, linen, velours, all for sunning suits, sometimes even for swimming. 'Whatever you wear for sunning, whatever fabric or colour,' said American *Vogue* in 1940, 'Don't sunbake all day in a suit with a fancy neckline. This is especially sinister when done the day of a party, because once you're branded, you're branded for some time.'

The complete beach kit, American style. A V 1948 Eric. *Brigance*

'Stripes can be a hazard or a joy. North-to-South ones slenderize, East-to-West ones, just the opposite: don't buy a striped suit just because Stripes are Being Worn!' A V 1940

1950

A V 1943 R.B. Willaumez. *Flexees*

Willaumez draws for American *Vogue*: the new, softer look in swimwear, both swimsuits and cover-ups. Flared skirts were viable in the United States, where fabric rationing was never over-stringent. These little knotted, tied, ruched tops and full skirts, fashionable in the United States throughout the War, swept Europe afterwards, in cottons, Hawaiian and exotic prints. Trousers, shorts, culottes in spun rayon, *opposite*, jacket in wool, soft and comfortable for sun-protection, tailored, worn with wedge-soled sandals, peon hats.

A V 1942
R.B. Willaumez

A V 1940
R.B. Willaum
*Left to right:
Best, Bonwit T
Peck & Peck*

AV 1940 André de Dienes. *Left to right: Stern's, Bonwit Teller*

'Mr and Mrs Ronald Reagan at Palm Springs,' *opposite*. 'Ronald Reagan was, before Hollywood, a sports reporter, NBC announcer. Mrs Reagan (Jane Wyman) – singer, storywriter. Their next picture is "Angel from Texas". They swim in Sharktex suits.' Hollywood swimwear in 1940, very tight indeed, some five inches of midriff now on display, skirt-like shorts tight across the upper thigh. Softer version, *this page above*, in celanese rayon jersey, Everfast piqué, more feminine, little-girl, fitting tightly only at the waist. New beach headgear, *this page right*: the kite-tail cap worn with fitting, zipped swimsuit in white piqué and Lastex, cut away at leg and back.

1940 Alexander Paal.
s of Hollywood

AV 1940 André de Dienes. *Brigance*

FV 1943 Keogh. *Jacques Heim*

By 1948 British and French *Vogue* editions were once again showing swimwear fashions throughout the early summer. Here, designer swimwear for summer 1948, drawn by Keogh. *This page*, amazing beach robe in vivid colours which trebled as cape, towel, even beach bag, called 'Guérite'. Street and beach clothes very much in line: the small waist, full skirt, *opposite second from right*, derived from the New Look. Trousers are way above the ankle, have turn-up cuffs and creases like men's, hats are low-crowned, huge, jackets to hip-length.

FV 1948 Keogh. *Le right: Maggy Rouff Jeanne Lafaurie, Lu Lelong, Maggy Rou Lucien Lelong, Jacq Griffe, Molyneux*

ACQUES HEIM

Two beach scenes with an air of danger. *Opposite*, stark tree stumps on the beach presage the years of barbed wire to come: this is British *Vogue*'s last swimwear feature until after the war. *This page*, Sea Island beach, patrolled by the 'sea horsemen' on dark horses. Swimsuits *opposite* in brightly printed Lastex with detachable skirts, matching towelling-lined coats. Two-piece *on this page*, much more sophisticated in black gabardine, halter-neck top, midriff on show.

OVERLEAF: Perfect tan, perfect figure, perfect bathing suit, *left*: the suit, worn here with optional sun-band, both as decoration and back protection, is 'a most exacting maillot', close-fitting, elegant, in navy-blue wool jersey. Floating peacefully in clear waters, *right*, another one-piece, the bodice in rayon jersey, the rest a combination of rayon and Lastex, its elastication making it kind to most figures.

AV 1948 Croner. *Brigance*

AV 1948 Rawlings. *Frances Sider*

AV 1944 Kay Bell. *Henri Bendel*

1950

'Travelling was once a weighty affair, but the new mechanics of it, the rocketing speeds and the shrinking fares, let us take it as lightly as the dandelion clock and go like the wind . . . there is an itch in *Vogue*'s soles as undeniable as anyone's.' The travel bug bit as hard in the fifties, after the Second World War, as it had in the twenties, after the First. Swimwear was photographed in 'real-life' situations in exotic settings like the Caribbean, Australia, Andalusia, Ireland, Yugoslavia, Scandinavia: models, fashion editor and photographer flown there by the national airline of the country. Quite naturally one of the important factors in choosing swimwear became the lightness, compactness, uncrushability, of the clothes which had to be transported long distances in a small space.

'The bathing suit has acquired a new state of – dress, not undress' (British *Vogue*, 1953). During the first half of the decade some of the smartest swimwear was not skin-tight, elasticated: it was unconstructed, gathered, rather like a child's romper suit. Bikinis, too, were less clinging; with emphasis on the bared midriff (some four or five inches now on display) and the bosom: covered with crossover bodice, or cuffed top. The look was *jeune fille* and unsophisticated.

White fringed playsuit with detachable looped piqué skirt. BV 1956 Lawrence Le Guay. *Dorville*

After 1955 the mood changed. A more calculated, feline look began to permeate the whole world of fashion. Models posed for the camera (and sometimes even with the camera, see pages 58 and 59), rather than appearing to be oblivious of its presence. Swimming costumes began once again to emphasize the body's curves, partly by revealing more of them: 'less suit's the idea – even maillots start lower on the bosom, stop high on the leg', said American *Vogue* in 1959 – but even more by making clever use of bias-cut, elasticated and special effect fabrics. The newest costumes now were strapless, with attachable straps for swimming: they were skin-tight, and some were even lightly boned to increase body-hugging effect, with (very) low necks, either V or rounded. The back of this type of costume was camisole-shaped, and on strapped suits the back was usually very low-cut. Waistline and bosom were focal points: the former emphasized by a matching or contrast belt, or simply by a seam in the suit, the latter by padded cups sewn in between two layers of fabric – or, again, by seaming.

Swimhats had been fashionable since the outset of the twentieth century. Now, in the fifties, they were at their most tailored, most extravagant. US Rubber produced a new fabric called water-velvet, which looked like cotton or nylon velvet, but was waterproof and stretchy. This was used to produce some of the prettiest headgear, brightly coloured, appliquéd with flowers, ribbons, contrasting bands of fabric, often designed by milliners. There was, however, a growing movement towards hatless swimming among the fashionable, and the end of the fifties saw the demise of the swimhat as a fashionable essential. During the seventies it reappeared in the wake of the

fitness craze, when the Speedo hat for competition swimming moved fleetingly into high fashion.

The fifties face for the beach was brightly painted: lips were matt pinks, reds, apricots, changing subtly from season to season; eyes too were emphasized, with dark tones, new waterproof colours, mascara, eyebrows artificially darkened. The skin itself was pale, protected from the sun by foundation and powder, shaded by parasols. These were very fashionable throughout the decade, in pastels and bright colours, and often matched beach outfits.

The cuffed bodice which was so popular for swimsuits during the early fifties was echoed in shorts and tops designed to be worn over them. Trousers, too, were often cuffed. 'Pretty print feminine versions of masculine garments', said British *Vogue* in 1952,' beach pyjamas (back again, their tapering trousers looking neat and new) and bush shirts are delightfully easy to wear on lazy days when even a crossword's a chore!' Dungarees, too, were adopted by women as beachwear, in cotton, linen, prints. Like trousers they were often cut off below the knee and were tight-fitting. Sleeveless shirts were an alternative to bush and man-tailored shirts. The sloppy joe was equally popular on and off the beach: it could be worn over a swimsuit, or with trousers or shorts. Big beach hats appeared again, in rougher straw than had been usual in the thirties: some had flat brims and high crowns, some had shaped brims, all were very soft and unstarched. Espadrilles were ever-present, and very flat leather thongs were worn right down to the water's edge.

New fabrics, and new methods of processing cotton, were perhaps the most important developments in swimwear during the fifties. Uncrushable cotton was now available: treated so that the clothes made from it would crease very little when folded and would drip dry (requiring minimum ironing) when washed. 'We're singing the praises, too, of the new, trouble-free fabrics – the drip-dry cottons, the Terylene, Orlon and nylon – that might have been invented just for holiday time, when clothes *must* stay crisp.' (British *Vogue*, 1956.) Satinized Lastex was the newest form of stretchy fabric; Lastex was woven with Lurex thread too. All shiny fabrics were fashionable: 'everglaze' cotton chintz and knitted, tightly spun (and thus iridescent) silks were used for swimsuits and playsuits. Prints were bold and bright; lots of Mexican, West African and West Indian designs were reproduced on cottons. Clear Madras checks and stripes of varying boldness, embroidered fabrics and Persian prints, added a touch of exotica to already bright, stark makeup and swimwear shapes.

1960

956 Rutledge.
*fo of Emme
, Rose Marie
* (suit)

VOGUE

SUMMER LEISURE

CLOTHES FOR SEA AND COUNTRY

THE ARTS—ON HOLIDAY

Models giving as good as they get: both equipped with the latest professional cameras. The Plexiglas-encased Leica on the left is designed, as is the hat, for water contact. This high fashion, milliner-designed hat was sponsored by US Rubber, using their new 'water-velvet'. The model, *right*, wears the essential one-piece swimsuit, seamed to reveal the figure. With it goes a fuchsia pink chiffon scarf, matching lipstick and nails – and no swimhat.

BV 1952 Penn

BV 1956 Helmut Newton. *Harvey Nichols*

Two of the sexiest swimsuits of the fifties, *left*: stopping high on the leg, low on the bosom, emphasizing the body's curves with perfect fit. That on the *left* is in the new satinized Lastex with boned top, on the *right* elasticized wool jersey, to be worn strapless or halter-necked. *Opposite*, two black and white suits in wool jersey, one herringboned, the other in banker's stripes, both very elegant yet without the same feline sophistication. Also on the contrast theme is this playsuit, *above*, in domino-spotted cotton with split personality. All the models wear the fashionably small, dark-toned sunglasses.

BV 1951 Don Honeyman. *Jaeger*

AV 1955 Rawlings. *Brigance, Jane Irwill*

A V 1959 Rutl
Tina Leser

Sun colours sunning themselves, *opposite*, pink and orange diamonded cotton with a halter top (more suntan showing than ever), elasticized shorts, in Everglaze cotton. Parasols, *this page*, became the essential beach accessory with the revival of the English Rose complexion. This large pink parasol provides the perfect defence against the sun's ageing rays, while the body is exposed. The subtle nuances in tone of lipstick were an important feature of beach presentation, setting off the pale, perfect features.

B V 1950 Penn

A V 1957 Prigent *to right Roxanne Rose Marie Reid Maurice Handler*

The cotton swimsuit, *left*, has stripes at right angles on the bodice and shorts. The model wears the perfect bathing makeup: waterproof eyeshadow creating heavy-lidded allure, brightly painted lips, polished nails. The three bathing beauties, *right*, wear suits with varied neck and strap lines. One of the most popular was the T-bar cut, despite the odd tan patterns which could result. The girl on the *left* models a neatly tailored, skirted costume striped in blue and green, like layers of sea water, emphasizing the curve of the hips and the waistline.

F V 1956 Prigent. *Corot*

957 Rutledge.
e Salon (right),
Fifth Avenue

The most elegant
mermaids, *opposite*:
sub-aqua ballerinas
in stage-like make-
up – in fact the
newest waterproof
colours for skin,
eyes, lips. The
swimhats are of US
Rubber's water-
velvet, which
stretched, clung to
the head, and could
be dyed bright
colours like this
clear pink. The
fabric flowers were
not submersible and
had to be snapped
off for swimming!
Stripy Lastex suit
with skirt, *this page*,
worn by a latter-
day Eve in tropical
Garden of Eden.

A V 1956 Coffin.
Catalina

1960

'The paragon figure . . . – fit and supple with a luxurious unhurried kind of tawniness – is Suzy Parker's' (American *Vogue*, 1964.) This softly feminine shape, not arch, not coy, but not kept hidden (as bikinis shrank and one-piece costumes grew briefer than ever), was the vogue until Twiggy's arrival at the end of the sixties. She, both in face and figure, voiced the tremendous change in fashion's emphasis, from the rounded and worldly-wise woman, to a girl who was unsophisticated, just out of her teens, still sharp at the edges, unselfconscious. Not only did the shape of clothes change to suit the new image: fashions were marketed as they were produced (rather than in strict seasons as previously), through the new small boutiques which had a fast turnover and sold everything necessary to the 'look' rather than having a speciality.

Swimwear reflects the changing mood. Swimsuits and bikinis of the early sixties were full of batiste and uplift (all-important underwiring for the bosom), to emphasize or create curves. By the end of the decade small bosoms were fashionable, and thus all the bolstering disappeared, leaving a natural look: costumes were cut with less curve, more severely shaped. A great variety of styles for bikinis and one-pieces appeared.

'The new way for a bikini,' said British *Vogue* in 1963, 'is little boy shorts, a built up bra': these were usually cut straight across the thigh, perhaps with a belt over the hips in patent, nautical-striped, or contrast fabric. The bra could be solid, like the top of a traditional maillot, but cut away at the midriff; or, it could be constructed from two semicircular cups held together with wide bands of fabric. By 1968 the picture had changed, and the bikini was now 'the minimum two piece for a perfect tan, leaving the least possible marks from sunbathing' (French *Vogue*, 1968). Bikini shorts were smaller, straight-cut or shaped over the thigh, the top formed from two triangles with narrow back and shoulder straps for maximum exposure to the sun, or a *bandeau*.

The one-piece suit changed shape, too: it became less rigid, more body-shaped with less or no additional padding or shaping. Newest version was the maillot on Courrèges' 'space-age' theme with circular cut-outs at sides or front and back. Some were bikini-like, held together only by a narrow

Susan Hampshire is a tiger on the sands in sensational tiger pullover with hood. B V 1964 David Bailey. *Slix*

Dark jersey romper suit with a soft drawstring neck. B V 1964 Helmut Newton. *Burgess Ledward*

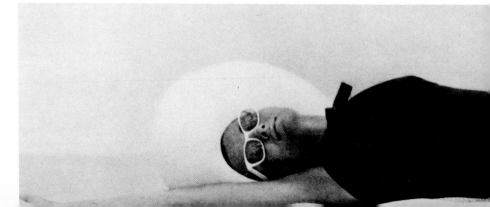

strip of fabric at centre back and front. Another new version was the 'jewel neckline' costume, the throat circled with a necklace of fabric, the body of the suit attached to it at front and back.

Fewer beach accessories were vital during this decade than previously. A towelling beach robe, however, was almost indispensable. Some were full length, but most were very mini, with wide boat necklines and roll collars, or zipped, with a hood. Dresses to throw over swimming togs were the simplest cut imaginable, two straight pieces of fabric tied together over the shoulders, or with little sleeves, but all easy, casual. Bright, stripy canvas, or even patent, beach bags carried costume, towel, throwover. Jewellery was often worn on the beach: huge earrings, gold chains around the waist, neck, wrist; shoes were out.

Fabric was all-important. New nylons appeared: 'the quick change maillot – when it's dried in the sun it's a sinuous velvety black, and when it's soaked with water it glistens like a seal on the rocks. In the miracle fibre Vyrene.' (British *Vogue*, 1965.) Prints were bold, huge dots, large geometric shapes, like the Mary Quant daisy logo, for example, and bold whorls in black and white (very popular) or very bright colours. Printing on nylon jersey was by now of a very high standard, and new dyes with new fixers permeated the fibre so deeply that the print remained bold when stretched. 'Wild jungle animals, not content with their invasion of the city, now propose to stalk the beaches too. The patterns are dappled into a skin of Bri-Nylon which is, after all, as sinuous and stretchy in its own way as the original skin.' (British *Vogue*, 1964.) These leopard and tigerskin prints were as popular for beach cover-ups and dresses as for swimwear: to make them fit still better, zig-zag stitching let seams stretch too. Others were open-weave-effect fabrics: *broderie anglaise* for tops and shirts, even bikinis; crochet still more popular for suits and cover-ups. Flower-power reached bikinis, and some had appliquéd daisies with realistic yellow centres, white petals. For jackets, capes, mini throwovers, towelling was the most widely used fabric and a stretchy version appeared. Pipings and bindings for all beachwear were bright and bold, in tune with the whole sixties look: vivid, casual 'costumes for better tans' (French *Vogue*, 1968).

Knitted jewel-neck swim-suit in graded rainbow colours. BV 1967 Bob Richardson. *Lil*

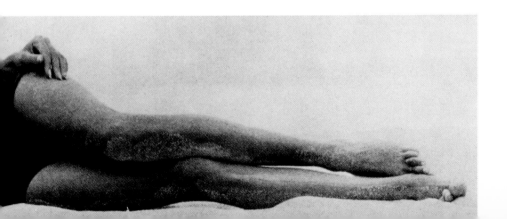

1970

AV 1964 Helmut Newton. *Samuel Robert*

New fabrics for swimwear in the sixties. *This page above*, ivory kidskin bikini, little bandeau cut straight across, short shorts riding low on the hipbone: all very supple, marvellously stark against the vivid gleam of wet-gold skin, in the setting of Ayers Rock, Australia. Flower-power influence in swimwear fashion, *right*: Marisa Berenson in flower-studded bikini, daisies made from cotton piqué embroidered onto organdie. This is the most popular bikini shape of the decade, brief top, deep knickers, hardly cut away over the hip.

FV 1968 Bob Richardson. *Tiktiner/Amie*

BV 1964 David Bailey.
Slix

On location, 1964. *This page*, in Las Palmas, in the middle of the film crew making 'Wonderful Life': stencil swimsuit for a strong suntan to draw round. Printed ocelot, it fits in front and is punched out at the back and sides. Racy black maillot, *opposite*, sleek, back-strapped, stripped down for maximum sun-tanning (the strap unbuttons and tucks out of sight, for still more exposure). Photographed at Wanda, near Sydney, the spear-fisherman-out-of-water is Australian champion Ron Taylor.

AV 1964 Helmut New
Brigance/Sinclair

FV 1967 David Bailey. *Drugstand*

B V 1969 Arnaud de Rosnay. *Tipper Ipper Appa*

The psychedelic sixties: *opposite*, 'Boo-Boo' fabric for minimum bikini top, strapless, with matching sawn-offs. The fabric design has an African flavour, raised flowers and leaves in black on a yellow ground. Suzy Parker, *this page right*, paragon figure of the decade, in confetti-printed pink bikini to wrap in a sarong skirt, shaded under a matching hat. The bikini·top, like that *opposite*, has the underwired, batiste-laden look of the sixties, the briefs deep at the sides. *Above* are beach jacket and wide trousers in stripes from a beach umbrella, made of crepe, in the bright, candy colours of fashion.

A V 1964 Bert Stern. *Lord & Taylor*

Smaller and smaller
bikinis as the seventies
approach. In spongy
Dropnyl Nylfrance,
opposite, for a very bare-
backed, triangular-cupped
bikini: very young,
carefree with its complete
lack of boning and batiste.
This page, electric,
elasticated satin bikini,
with scooped-out neck-
line at front and back,
tiny briefs, gold chain
around the waist.

F V 1969 Jeanloup Sieff.
Pascal

Fashion's emphasis in the early sixties had been on a mature woman, rounded and sophisticated. Now, in the late sixties, this changed and the woman in focus was younger, still sharp at the edges both emotionally and physically. *Opposite*, tiny bikini-bottom in open crochet over slim hips, the skin evenly bronzed to perfection. The first dip of the season, *this page*, in crochet suit, skinny, low-cut, bright, young.

FV 1968 Franco Rubartelli.
Café des Arts

1970

Seventies playsuit in Tricel jersey, cross-strapped over the back with big white buttons. B V 1971 Hans Feurer. *Copper Coin/Just Looking*

Ingrid Boulting in a cotton shirred bikini of brightly coloured checks. B V 1971 David Bailey. *Pascal*

'Bright little strips of bathing suits with new twists and ties, ready now to make you look marvellous, to give the body every chance for sun benefits – new beauty, and health, and glow. . . .' (American *Vogue*, 1971.)

Hair and skin had to be in peak condition, muscles in tone, for exposure in swimwear. The body was in fashion, particularly on the beach, and there was no doubt in anyone's mind that the swimsuit, however delicious, was merely a frame for it. The picture inside glowed and glistened with health – and the latest sun preparation. Key summer jargon words for choosing these were 'protection' and 'tanning factor' (this was a number given to most sun preparations to denote the degree of protection from the sun's rays each gave). Beauty houses vied with each other to produce creams and oils to speed up the tanning process artificially and to cater for the greatest variety of skin types and sensitivities.

In 1971, bathing suits and bikinis were 'like bright body sandals – stripped over slick, glowing skin' (American *Vogue*). Bikinis were still boyish, with straight-cut, scarcely shaped bikini pants and tops like abbreviated tank tops (tight-fitting, scoop-necked, sleeveless jerseys), bandeaux, or little triangular cups. Bathing one-pieces, too, started the decade in a rather solid form. All swimwear gradually lost coverage, gained shock appeal, feel appeal, as new soft and shiny fabrics were used. Halter necks were the most popular top shape for all swimwear mid-decade. Bikinis were, by now, minuscule: tiny bikini pants held together over the hipbones by perhaps an inch of fabric, or rouleau ties (which could be undone for perfect suntanning), were the norm. Tops were small, too, with fabric gathered into a centre-front knot or ring, detachable halter or shoulder straps.

British *Vogue* sighted 'the smallest bikini on any horizon' in 1975, but the daring were no longer wearing teeny weeny bikinis: they were removing them, at least the top half, on all the leading beaches of the world (though

Brigitte Bardot and her set had been doing this for years at Saint-Tropez). In Britain, even, Brighton was to declare part of its beach a nudist area in 1980.

But swimwear did have a future, for not everyone wanted to expose themselves unclad; in addition, it was proved, by the end of the decade, that exposure to the sun could be dangerous. The majority of the decade had belonged to the bikini, but during the last few years the one-piece suit regained the importance it had maintained in the thirties. The most popular type of suit was a close relative of the leotard. Exercises of all kinds were fashionable in the seventies: dancing and fitness classes part of every smart woman's régime. Leotards designed for these could even be worn for swimming, particularly when made from Lycra, which reacted equally well to stretching wet or dry. Generally, however, heavier weights of knit fabric were used for swimwear, strappier styles with camisole tops, low V necks, added frills around neck, or ruching down the centre front or sides. The trademark of the years up to 1980 was the very high cut of bikinis and one-pieces over the upper thigh and pelvis, in some cases to the waist, exposing the hipbones. In addition to these shapes derived from the maillot and the leotard, there was a breed of 'fantasy' suits, cut in strange shapes, rather unconstructed, strips of fabric held together with straps and rings, all in shiny, elastic, ruched fabrics: some were for swimming, some were *maillots de soir* which could be worn alone or with trousers or skirts.

'Simply wizard playsuits. Sundresses with slightly flared shorts. Plenty of straps crossing bare backs. Lots and lots of buttons. Super colours. Cotton, crepe and jersey' (British *Vogue*, 1971). Reminiscent of the beach suits of the forties and fifties, these had a 'little-girl' air about them and could be worn alone or over a swimsuit. But by mid-decade they had disappeared, and the only really popular beach throwovers were shirts, perhaps knotted around the waist, and button-through or wrapover dresses, casually thrown over a swimsuit and left unfastened: the suit, tailored and sleek, was a complete 'look' in itself.

The overwhelming impression of swimwear in the seventies was of bright, bright tones and lots of shine. Matt colours were used at the outset of the decade, but glossy fabrics, once considered vulgar even for the beach, took over as high fashion. Lycra swimwear started only in the most expensive ranges, reaching the lower echelons of the market by 1980. It could be treated to shine like a healthy second skin, to glisten or sparkle (or even remain matt), and fitted more tightly than a glove to hold in bulges. Soft fabrics were used for swimwear too: stretch towelling, wool-look jersey, knitted in soft ribbing and pretty stitches, silk for shirts and dresses, or cotton. Stripes, broad and narrow, abounded; two or three-tone suits, too, particularly with white, for business-like amateur or professional surfing and diving suits which were sleek and bright enough to be seen mid-breaker.

Tiny bikini.
BV 1975 Petito Galvez

1980

976 Barbieri.
éar

Bathing suits like
bright body sandals.
Opposite, the most
erotic sea-hunter's
outfit – bright
Lurex hooded
maillot, revealing
the whole leg and
buttocks glistening
with sun-oil. Over
the suit, silk chiffon
print cloak by Issey
Miyake. *This page*,
very cutaway suit,
backless, with gold
straps, worn with
reflector sunglasses
with the 1978
downward slope.

FV 1978 Jacques
Malignon. *Arabel*

1971 Carrara. *Pascal*

Midriff glimpses, fit for the sun. Two very simple bikinis: the emphasis now on a solid block of cover, shaped by the body's contours, maximum exposure. The bikini, *opposite*, is of Lycra, with horizontal centre seam on the bra, giving subtle shaping, that on *this page*, of ribbed Antron nylon. The fashionable shape is rounded, but fit, tanned, hair shiny with health.

AV 1971 Penn. *B. H. Wragge*

The bathing suits to wear when you're wishing you had the freedom-feeling of no bathing suit at all: the extra-super-ultra thin suits, nothing but marvellous colour. *Above left*, bright skin of Antron nylon and Lycra scooped low at neck, high over hips. No darts at all in the tank suit *below left*, wonderful for a wonderful figure. *Centre*, oldest, latest fashion of all – nudity.

AV 1975 Penn. *Gottex of Israel (below), Roxanne (above).*

IV 1974 Arthur Elgort. G. *Alberti*

Softest swimsuit, *above*, very cutaway, low, in ribbed Scintex:
one of the first anti-aquatic (needed hand-washing) *maillots de
soir* in the seventies. *Left*: weird, threatening setting for the
whole range of swimwear available. Over everything, *far left,
second from left*, easy, pretty, crinkle cotton smock, simple
silky black shirt. Strapless bikini, *centre*, the best friend of an
even suntan, the top pulled into a ring centrally. A serious-
swimming maillot, *second from right*, with bare back, next to a
striped-and-solid bikini for sunning and swimming alike.

A V 1975 Deborah Turbeville. *Left to right: Amerikan Climax,
Jantzen (2), Catelina (2)*

BV 1976 David
Bailey. *Hamilton
Cruise*

Swimwear in exotic
settings: *this page*,
canary-bright
stretch towelling
playsuit and royal
blue tights on a
tropical sand dune.
Opposite, in Crete,
deep blue sea, sky,
swimsuit in Lycra:
gathered centre
front, 1979-style,
crêpe de chine robe
thrown over it.

BV 1979 Mik
Reinhardt.
Strawberry St

Sultry, sexy, shiny 'one-pieces'
from three designers. More for
show than action, they reveal and
frame the body, and are more
suitable for the boudoir, or for
glittering evenings with skirt and
diamonds, than for mornings on
the beach with sunhat and towel.
Fabrics from *left to right* are bronzed
cotton, Lycra with appliqué,
gilded Lycra; bodies glisten too.

FV 1979 Helmut Newton. *Left to
right: Yves Saint-Laurent, Ted
Lapidus, Yves Saint-Laurent,
Scherrer (2)*

1980 Bruce Weber.
Bruce/Regine

Two-tone contrasts:
white, pastels with
dark tones. One-
shoulder red and white
swimsuit, *opposite*,
brief enough to catch
the sun, firm enough to
surf in, particularly
when protected by the
bronzed lifesavers at
Bondi Beach. Another
suit on simple, clean-
cut lines, *this page*,
peachy cotton one-
piece, cut away over
the hip, worn with
black ciré nylon
raincoat, rolled up and
disguised as shirt.

BV 1978
Alex Chatelain.
*Jean-Charles de
Castelbajac*

Black and white: graphic design chequerboard and tiny checks for this camisole-top one-piece, at the outset of the eighties. IV 1980 Peter Lindbergh. *Armonia*